Character Education, Grades 5–6

Character Education Grades 5–6
Introduction

Character is the inner nature of a person. It determines how a person thinks, feels, and acts. Given the fundamental importance of character, it is vital that we teach our children the values that will enable them to make decisions that better themselves, their community, and the world.

This program is designed to assist you in developing these positive character traits. The six basic traits targeted in *Character Education* are: caring, fairness, trustworthiness, responsibility, respect, and citizenship. The teaching of these traits follows the standards established by the Character Education Partnership (CEP). The stories and activities can be integrated into the curriculum as a supplemental source that promotes a strong character foundation as prescribed by the Partnerships in Character Education Pilot Project.

Organization

There are seven units, six based on one of the core character traits. The last unit is a wrap-up unit that covers all six traits. Each unit focuses on a story that exhibits the trait or traits. Follow-up activities develop understanding and provide a context for application. The units incorporate the following elements:

Teacher Information: This page defines the core character trait and lists the qualities of that trait in language that students can understand. It also summarizes the story and briefly offers suggestions for introducing the activity pages. Finally, the page outlines a group project to be completed over the course of study as well as a list of books to further support the teaching of the character trait.

Story: The story selections introduce the character trait and serve as a model. The selections are high interest and on grade level. They provide an excellent point of departure for discussion, especially through the "Think and Talk" question at the end of each story. Moreover, they represent a variety of genres for easy integration into a language arts curriculum.

Story Response: The story response page has five questions. The first two are comprehension questions that relate directly to the story. The third and fourth questions ask students to reflect on the character trait. The last question asks students how they demonstrate that trait in their daily life.

Activities: The follow-up activities focus on the basic qualities that make up each trait. These activities are fun, interesting, and varied enough to engage students, thereby increasing participation and learning. Many activities are open-ended in order to challenge all learners and encourage success.

The first activity following the story response is to be used in conjunction with the theme bulletin board. It asks students to notice when their classmates exhibit one of the targeted traits, such as fairness, caring, or respect. Using the cutouts that correspond to each trait, students write the names of the classmates who demonstrated good character as well as a brief summary of what they observed. The students then hang the cutouts on the theme bulletin board.

The remaining activities can be used in multiple curriculum areas. Some encourage writing, making charts, drawing, or playing a game.

Use

To begin, determine the implementation that best fits your students' needs and your classroom structure. The following plan suggests a format for this implementation:

In advance, prepare a classroom bulletin board that displays the character symbol and lists the qualities. You may also wish to photocopy the blackline masters on the back of the pull-out activity cards to pass out to students.

1. Introduce the core character trait. Lead a discussion of the character symbol and how it represents the trait.

2. Read the story. Follow each story with a class discussion identifying how the story represents the trait. Encourage students to share what they learn from the story.

3. Complete the story response.

4. Pass out the first activity related to the bulletin board. Explain that students should look for examples of the targeted trait during the course of the unit. When the unit is complete, remove the cutouts from the bulletin board and pass them out to the students whose names are on them. You may wish to provide a treat for anyone whose name is shown.

5. Remaining activities can be implemented as time permits.

Additional Notes

Character Symbol: Each character trait is represented with a graphic tree symbol to serve as a visual cue and reminder. These symbols appear on the corresponding unit pages, activity card posters, blackline masters, and awards.

Parent Letter: Send the Letter to Parents home with students.

Interview: During each unit, have students choose a person who they think exemplifies the character trait. Have students use the form on page 58 to interview that person.

Self-Assessment: Students can use page 59 to tell when they have demonstrated good character. You may wish to ask them to complete a form daily, weekly, or over the course of the unit.

Calendar: The calendar on page 60 can be used for a wide range of unit activities, such as recording good character behavior or logging assignments in order to encourage responsible work habits.

Awards: Individual character awards can be found on pages 61–63. You may wish to make copies of them and give them to students to recognize and reinforce good character behavior.

Activity Card Posters: Four-color posters showing the character symbols can be found in the back of the book. It is highly recommended that you display on a bulletin board the poster showing the symbol, as several activities are related to it.

Blackline Masters: Blackline masters showing the symbol and listing each quality can be found on the back of the activity card posters. You may wish to make copies for students to color and take home during the unit. These blackline masters can also be used as covers for individual, group, or class books. Each child or group contributes writing or art about character. Then, the pages are assembled into book form, with the blackline masters as the covers.

Dominoes: Cut out the individual domino pieces for students to play in an activity center. Up to three players begin with five dominoes. They should match words to a symbol. Other uses might include: students draw a domino to determine the group they will work in; students draw a domino and identify one quality associated with the word or symbol; students play concentration, forming word or picture pairs.

Dear Parent,

As parents and teachers, we try to teach our children basic manners and values in order to help them become respected and productive members of the family and community. These values emphasize the character traits we wish to impart to our children. A strong character based on ethical values can help children make the right choices when faced with difficult situations. With the events of the past years, it is even more important that we work together to prepare our children to take their places in an increasingly complex world. If we prepare them adequately, our children will be able to make decisions that benefit themselves, their community, and the world.

During the year, your child will learn about the six core traits of character: caring, fairness, trustworthiness, respect, responsibility, and citizenship. From time to time, I may send home activity pages. Some of these may have been completed in class, while others are to be completed at home. To reinforce the importance of character growth and development, please consider the following suggestions:

- Together, go over the completed work your child brings home.

- For assignments that are to be completed at home, provide your child a place to work, and then review the work when it is finished.

- Encourage your child to explain the basic qualities of the character trait being studied.

- Point out ways your child, family members, or community members exhibit the qualities.

- Offer praise when your child shows the character trait.

- Inquire about the progress of the group project.
  (You might even like to help!)

Thank you for your help. Your child and I appreciate your assistance and reinforcement in this learning process.

Cordially,

Caring

Caring is one of the basic traits of character. It is the true and honest concern for others. Most people are genuine in their spirit of love and giving. However, some caring can be a disguise for giving with the expectation of getting something in return. Stress to students the difference in giving to get something in return and giving because it makes others—and the giver—feel good.

The basic qualities of caring include:
- Help and comfort those in need.
- Be kind and considerate to all.
- Thank those who do a kindness.
- Forgive those who are mean or thoughtless.
- Give to others in time and money—charity—to make their life better.

About the Symbol

For students, the most obvious way to show caring is to help and comfort those in need. In many cultures, food is given to others in times of joy and sorrow. The basket of apples represents providing food when someone is busy or ill, showing that someone took extra time and thought to care for another person.

About the Story (pages 6–8)

Hittin' Taters by Pam Zollman
Quan's baseball team needs a hitter like Travis, but Travis doesn't have money for a uniform, and he has to take care of his family's vegetable garden. The team pitches in to help tend the garden and sell vegetables to solve both problems.

About the Activities

Activity 1: Caring—A Class Act (page 9)

If possible, provide an apple snack for the class. Lead students in a discussion of how the apple can be a symbol for caring. Encourage them to be creative in their responses. Next, remind students to use the apples to recognize when classmates show caring behavior throughout the unit. You may wish to provide a special treat for students whose names appear on the apples.

Activity 2: Thanks for Caring (page 10)

Explain that caring involves showing and expressing thanks when someone shows a kindness. Then, review the parts of a friendly letter.

Activity 3: Caring in the Cafeteria (page 11)

Brainstorm with students what it means to be considerate. Spend some time talking about peer pressure and the importance of accepting differences. Then, invite students to share examples of times they showed consideration to someone who was different.

Group Project

Discuss with students the idea of charity—using time and money to help community members. Then, brainstorm a list of community groups that might need help, such as a senior citizens' home or a food bank. Guide students to choose, plan, and complete a project to help one of the groups.

At-home

Ask students to find ways that family members care for one another.

Related Reading

The Chronicles of Narnia by C. S. Lewis
The Incredible Journey by Sheila Burnford
The Miracle Tree by Christobel Mattingley

Hittin' Taters

by Pam Zollman

Quan frowned as he watched his team at batting practice. "You know what we need?" he asked.

"Someone who can slug the baseball," Bryan said.

"We need Travis. Remember all those homers he hit during gym class?" Quan asked.

Bryan picked up a bat. "Too bad he can't play this summer."

"Yeah, no time or money," Quan said.

Quan knew that Travis had lived on a farm with his parents. When Travis's father died, his mother had to sell the farm to pay debts. They moved into the house across from Quan. Travis and his mother didn't have much money, so they grew their own vegetables to cut food costs.

Taking a practice swing, Bryan said, "We could really use him."

As Quan walked home after practice, he decided to talk to Travis. There had to be a way for Travis to play on the team.

He found Travis in the backyard, competently weeding the huge garden. Quan could see ripening vegetables on some plants. Other plants were only tender shoots. Those all looked like weeds to Quan. Travis knew the difference, though.

"You're a regular grocery store," Quan exclaimed. "Squash, beans, lettuce, tomatoes, cucumbers, peppers, and more!"

Standing up, Travis brushed the dirt from his knees. "You can have some vegetables," he said. "We've got more than we need."

"Thanks." Quan picked several tomatoes. "Listen, Travis," he said finally, "we really want you on our team."

Travis looked away, embarrassed. "Someone has to weed, water, and harvest the vegetables. That someone is me. Besides, I don't have the money for a uniform."

"If I found a way to solve those problems, would you play?" asked Quan.

"I'd love to," Travis said, "but I don't see how. Not this year."

"I'll find a way," Quan promised.

But as he walked out of Travis's backyard, he wasn't so sure. Travis's neighbor, Mrs. Elderwood, waved to Quan as he left.

"My, those are lovely tomatoes," she called out.

Quan held one up. "Travis grew them."

"That lad is quite industrious," she said. "But I don't think he's enjoying summer. He should be playing baseball with his friends."

Quan looked at her curiously. Had she overheard them?

"I don't like store-bought tomatoes," she continued. "They're as hard as baseballs! I'd rather buy fresh vegetables like these."

"Thanks," Quan said. "You've given me an idea!" He ran home to call his teammates.

The next day, the entire team met in Travis's backyard.

"Here's the plan," Quan announced as Travis watered the plants. "We'll sell extra vegetables to friends, family, and neighbors. You'll make enough money to buy a uniform."

"Great!" Travis said. "But the problem is only half solved."

"We're the other half," Bryan explained. "Coach Williams emphasizes the importance of teamwork. Well—here's the team. Put us to work!"

"Who knows?" Quan said. "Weeding may strengthen our arm muscles so we'll hit like you. First we'll harvest vegetables. Then we'll harvest homers."

"We'll be hittin' taters!" Bryan laughed. "That's what baseball players call home runs."

Travis beamed. "How can a guy turn down an offer like that?"

"He can't," said Quan. "Welcome to the team!"

⟫ Think and Talk ⟪

What is caring? How do the people in the story show caring?

Story Response

Directions

Answer the questions.

CARING

1. What does it mean to be considerate? How was Quan considerate of Travis?

   _____

   _____

2. Why is the help that the team gives Travis NOT a form of charity?

   _____

   _____

3. People show caring by helping. What are some other ways people show caring?

   _____

   _____

4. Why is it important to help others?

   _____

   _____

   _____

   _____

5. What are some ways that you show caring in school and at home?

   _____

   _____

   _____

Name _____ Date _____

Caring–A Class Act

CARING

One way to show caring is to be kind and considerate.

 **Directions**

Look for ways your classmates show caring. On an apple, write the name of a classmate and tell how he or she showed caring. Then, hang the apple on the tree.

Name

Name

Name

Name

Name _____ Date _____

Thanks for Caring

One way to show caring is to thank someone for his or her help.

 **Directions**

Think of a time recently when someone helped you. Write a letter to that person thanking him or her.

Name _____ Date _____

Caring in the Cafeteria

CARING

A considerate person is thoughtful of a person's rights and feelings.

 **Directions**

Look at the picture. Identify the ways that people are NOT being considerate. How can each situation be corrected?

_____

_____

_____

_____

_____

_____

_____

_____

Fairness

Fairness is the character trait that values equality, impartiality in making decisions, and willingness to correct mistakes quickly. It can be a difficult concept for young people to understand at times; however, even young children can learn the importance of treating people equally.

The basic qualities of fairness include:
- Take turns and share.
- Treat people equally.
- Be open-minded and listen.
- Do not blame people carelessly.
- Do not take advantage of people.
- Let consequences fit the wrongful act.

About the Symbol

Many heated discussions take place at school where children are developing group-involvement skills. Free time, in particular, can be especially difficult because there is little structure or guidance. This is when children can really show their developing awareness of why it is important to be fair. The tree with the two balanced swings serves as a reminder that fairness means treating people equally, sharing, and keeping an open mind.

About the Story (pages 13–15)

Thurgood Marshall: Supreme Court Justice
   by Robin Booth
The article tells about Thurgood Marshall's work to establish integration in American schools.

About the Activities

Activity 1: A Fair Swing (page 16)
Invite volunteers to share situations in which they felt they were treated unfairly. Ask those students what would have made the situation fair. Then, invite students to speculate why the swing is the symbol for the character trait of fairness. Remind the class to look for ways that their classmates show fairness in the classroom *and* on the playground. You may wish to

provide a small treat for students whose names appear on the swings.

Activity 2: Puzzled About Fairness (page 17)
Explain to students that a rebus puzzle is one that uses a combination of pictures and words to express a thought. Demonstrate the sentence, "I ate cookies" by drawing the following:

8   + ies

Activity 3: Fair or Foul? (page 18)
Lead students in a discussion of good sportsmanship. Invite them to share why being fair is part of being a good sport. Then, introduce the concept of compromise.

Group Project

Divide students into six groups. Assign each group one of the qualities of fairness listed above. Encourage them to think how the quality pertains to a school situation. Then, have the group create a poster that represents the quality they chose. Allow students to hang the posters in the school hallways.

At-home

Ask students to draw a picture of a conflict they had with a brother or sister. Encourage them to bring the picture to school and tell how the situation was resolved.

Related Reading

Harriet Tubman: Conductor on the Underground Railroad by Ann Petry
Holes by Louis Sachar
The Watsons Go to Birmingham—1963
   by Christopher Paul Curtis

Thurgood Marshall: Supreme Court Justice

by Robin Booth

FAIRNESS

Thurgood Marshall passed through the entrance of the United States Supreme Court at First and East Capital Streets, N.E., in Washington, D.C. Above the doorway, etched in stone, were the words, "Equal Justice Under the Law." He paused to read them and smiled. For so many years those words did not mean the same for white people and African Americans. There was no "Equal Justice" as far as African Americans were concerned. But today history would be made, he thought.

The Justices called on the confident African-American lawyer to present his case. For years he had planned and waited for a case like this. Other cases he had tried had prepared him well. He believed strongly in what he had to say. The name of this case was *Brown versus the Board of Education of Topeka, Kansas*, and it dealt with school segregation.

The year was 1954. White children and African-American children did not attend the same schools. This was the law. Thurgood did not think this was fair for the African-American children because often their schools were inferior. Their materials were old, their school buildings were run down, and their desks were not as good as those of the white children. Thurgood argued before the court that because of these discrepancies, segregated education was not equal education, and the law guaranteed equal education for all.

Thurgood was well-prepared and gave many examples. He cited psychological studies that said that African-American children felt inferior because of the inferior manner in which they were educated. He said that African-American children were placed at a disadvantage, and this was not fair to them—it was not what the law promised. The Supreme Court unanimously agreed. Thurgood won the case, so now children of all races could attend the same schools.

Unfortunately, schools were not immediately integrated. The Court had said in its ruling that the states must integrate the schools "with all deliberate speed." Many states took a long time to start the process of integrating the classrooms, while others did absolutely nothing toward doing what the Court had ordered. Thurgood continued the fight for integration and filed case after case to force school districts to do what the Supreme Court had ruled. Meanwhile, he worked other cases to end discrimination in voting, housing, criminal procedure, and public places.

In 1967 President Johnson asked Thurgood Marshall to serve as a Supreme Court Justice. He became the first African American to hold a seat on the high court. It was an appropriate position for a man who had done so much in his life to guarantee "Equal Justice Under the Law."

Think and Talk

What is fairness? How did the Supreme Court's ruling in the *Brown versus the Board of Education of Topeka, Kansas*, affect all schools and children?

Story Response

FAIRNESS

Directions

Answer the questions.

1. Why did Thurgood Marshall believe that segregated education was not equal under the law?

   _____

   _____

2. What was significant about President Johnson appointing Thurgood Marshall as a Supreme Court Justice?

   _____

   _____

3. What is prejudice? Why is a prejudiced person not fair?

   _____

   _____

4. How does receiving an equal opportunity relate to fairness?

   _____

   _____

   _____

5. Tell about a disagreement you had with a friend. How did you solve the problem? Was the solution fair? Explain.

   _____

   _____

   _____

A Fair Swing

A fair person treats everyone the same, no matter how they look, act, talk, or think. A fair person also takes turns and shares.

FAIRNESS

Directions

Look for ways that your classmates show fairness. Write the name of a classmate on a swing and tell about the fair action. Then, hang the swing on the tree.

Name

Name

Puzzled About Fairness

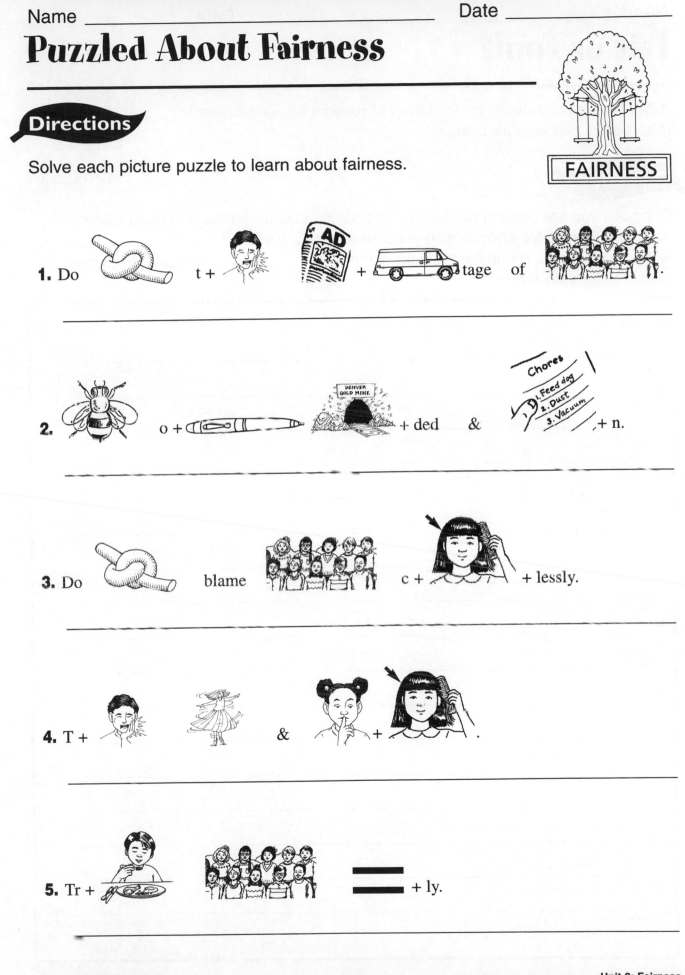

Directions

Solve each picture puzzle to learn about fairness.

1. Do [knot] t + [crying face] + [AD] + [van] tage of [group of people].

2. [bee] o + [pen] + [Denver Gold Mine] + ded & [Chores: 1. Feed dog, 2. Dust, 3. Vacuum] + n.

3. Do [knot] blame [group of people] – c + [girl combing hair] + lessly.

4. T + [crying face] [dancer] & [shushing person] + [girl combing hair].

5. Tr + [eating] [group of people] = + ly.

Name _____   Date _____

Fair or Foul?

A fair person is careful to get the facts and consider what other people think before making a decision.

FAIRNESS

Directions

Suppose you are playing basketball with some classmates. As you head toward the basket with the ball, another player accuses you of traveling (moving with the ball without dribbling). You insist that you did not travel. Write a paragraph about how you would solve the problem fairly.

Trustworthiness

A trustworthy person is honest, reliable, and loyal. This means always telling the truth, even when it is difficult. A trustworthy person can be relied upon to fulfill his or her commitments. Trustworthiness also means being loyal to friends and family members. This last concept, loyalty, can be hard for students. Loyalty to friends may cause students to feel caught between friends and what is morally right. This is especially true in regard to keeping secrets. Stress to students the difference between good and harmful secrets. Lastly, explain to students that trust is built up over time and that once it is broken, it can be hard to rebuild.

The basic qualities of trustworthiness include:
- Support your family and friends.
- Tell the truth.
- Do what you say you will do.
- Be on time.
- Keep secrets that do not harm others.
- Do what is right, even if it is hard to do.

About the Symbol

The basic qualities of trustworthiness are easy for students to understand. However, practicing them can be more of a challenge. The tree itself is a symbol to stand straight, strong, and firm in words and actions. The group of trees represents being loyal to family members and friends.

About the Story (pages 20–23)

Erron's Decision by Gus Gedatus
Erron doesn't tell anyone when a kite he flies damages a neighbor's tree. Erron faces another important decision when his baseball breaks a window and a lamp in another neighbor's house.

About the Activities

Activity 1: Tree-ific Trustworthiness (page 24)
Review the qualities of trustworthiness with students. Then, assign partners. Ask each partner to complete the activity page describing the ways his or her partner shows trustworthiness. Have students hang the trees on the theme bulletin board.

Activity 2: Trustworthy Advice (page 25)
Remind students that Sarah in *Erron's Decision* was willing to keep a secret, for a price. Ask students if Sarah demonstrated good character. Have them explain their answers. Next, lead students in a discussion of good and harmful secrets. Emphasize how to distinguish the difference between the two. You may wish to extend the activity by posing other ethical dilemmas.

Activity 3: Support and Trust (page 26)
Ask students to define *support*. Then, have them identify how Erron's dad supported him in the story. (He helped Erron board up the Kinsons' window and had a talk show about the topic of "Foolish Things I Did When I Was a Kid.") Next, discuss ways students can show support, such as attending a sibling's sports event, listening when a friend is hurt, or helping a busy parent do chores.

Group Project

Divide students into six groups. Assign each group one of the qualities of trustworthiness listed above. Have them write a skit that reflects the quality. Provide simple props for the students to use when they present the skit.

At-home

Remind students that part of being trustworthy is to complete homework and to turn it in on time. Encourage students to keep a homework log to help them track assignments.

Related Reading

The Lemonade Trick by Scott Corbett
The Secret Garden by Frances Hodgson Burnett
What Jamie Saw by Carolyn Coman

Erron's Decision
by Gus Gedatus

TRUSTWORTHINESS

Erron Harmon's father is a broadcaster for station KTUV, a radio station in a small town. Everyone knows Mr. Harmon, and everyone knows that Erron is his son. That's okay with Erron, because Erron thinks his dad is great. He hopes to be a radio host one day, too. Besides, Erron has learned to live with the ups and downs of being well-known.

Last year Erron's fame helped him learn a lesson. He and his friend Stephen bought a box kite. Neither of them had ever flown a kite before. Erron's dad said they should fly it in a wide-open space. They should have listened to him.

The boys flew the kite from Erron's front yard. It climbed quickly and looked wonderful. Then the wind changed. Before Erron could pull the kite back, it swerved into a crab-apple tree in Mrs. Lumke's yard. Mrs. Lumke was a prize-winning gardener with a huge, pink-flowering tree.

"We should have gone to the park," Erron told his friend. The boys climbed the tree to get the kite. Great clouds of pink flowers fell onto the lawn. They got the kite, but the tree had become much less pink. The boys went home, not knowing that Mrs. Lumke had been watching from her kitchen window.

Erron's dad has a talk show called "Town Talk." People call in to talk about the news. They don't talk about important news exclusively. Sometimes people just share stories about what's going on in town.

Mrs. Lumke called in to Mr. Harmon's talk show. She told the whole listening audience about his son, the kite, and the crab-apple tree. Other people started calling in with complaints about other kids and with "parenting advice."

Erron was grounded for a week. He had lots of time to think about what he had done. His dad told him that accidents happen, but he should have told Mrs. Lumke the truth about the kite instead of just leaving her tree and yard a mess. Erron felt bad about the embarrassment he had caused. He knew he had done a very foolish thing. He didn't know what to do except to try not to do anything so foolish again.

A week later, Erron was practicing his fast ball against an alley wall. The ball hit a corner of the wall and then flew off to the side. It crashed through a window and broke a lamp in the Kinsons' dining room. He knew that the Kinsons were out of town. However, Sarah Felty, who was out walking her dog, saw the whole thing.

"Nice going, Erron. Always showing off," Sarah snickered. Erron was mute. What could he say?

"I could call your father's talk hotline. Or ... maybe not. What will you give me?" she asked.

"What do you mean? Money?"

"Sure. Don't you get an allowance?"

"Let me think about it, okay?" Erron said. He thought, *Maybe I could give her my allowance, just for a couple of weeks.*

Erron sat on the back step. He didn't like the idea of evading the truth by paying someone to keep secrets. On the other hand, he didn't want people to call his dad about the son who always got into trouble.

Then Erron thought, *What would Dad do in this situation? What choice would he make?* The answer was easy. His dad would tell the truth, and that's exactly what Erron decided to do.

Erron called his dad and told him what had happened. That evening, Erron called Mrs. Lumke. He made a long overdue apology about the kite and her crab-apple tree. Then Erron and his dad boarded up the Kinsons' window. Later in the week, after the family arrived home, Erron apologized to them. He even contributed eight weeks' allowance to pay for the window and the lamp.

The next week the subject of "Talk Town" was "Foolish Things I Did When I Was a Kid." As Erron listened, he realized that he, too, had a story to tell. Maybe he would call in. Wouldn't his dad be surprised—especially when he told how his dad had helped him solve a problem with kites and crab-apple trees and fast balls and windows!

Think and Talk

What is trustworthiness? How did Erron break his father's trust? How did he regain it?

Story Response

TRUSTWORTHINESS

Directions

Answer the questions.

1. Which qualities of trustworthiness does Erron show in the story?

_____

_____

2. Part of trustworthiness is to keep secrets that do not harm others. Was Sarah being trustworthy when she offered to keep Erron's accident a secret? Explain.

_____

_____

3. What kind of secrets should be kept? Give examples.

_____

_____

4. What kind of secrets should be shared and with whom? Give examples.

_____

_____

5. Are you trustworthy? Give one example that shows you are a trustworthy person.

_____

_____

Name _____ Date _____

Tree-ific Trustworthiness

TRUSTWORTHINESS

A trustworthy person is a good friend or family member. The person fulfills his or her commitments.

Directions

Work with a partner. Think about one way the partner is trustworthy. Write about it on the tree. Then, glue your tree and your partner's tree beside each other on another sheet of paper.

_____
Name

_____

_____

_____

_____

_____

_____

_____

_____

Name _____ Date _____

Trustworthy Advice

TRUSTWORTHINESS

A trustworthy person helps family and friends. But sometimes it is hard to be loyal to the people that one cares about. There are times when a trustworthy person must choose between being loyal and doing what is right.

Directions

Suppose you are the advice columnist for the school newspaper. You receive the letter below. What advice will you give? Write a letter in response.

Dear West Oak Advice Writer,

I saw my best friend take a special ink pen out of a classmate's backpack. My friend said that if I was a good friend, I would not tell. I do not want to lose my best friend. What should I do?

Sincerely,
Adam

_____

_____

_____

_____

_____

_____

_____

_____

_____

_____

_____

Support and Trust

Trustworthy people are supportive. This means they encourage the people they care about. It also means that they stand up for their friends and family.

Directions

Write the names of three family members or friends. Then, tell how you support them.

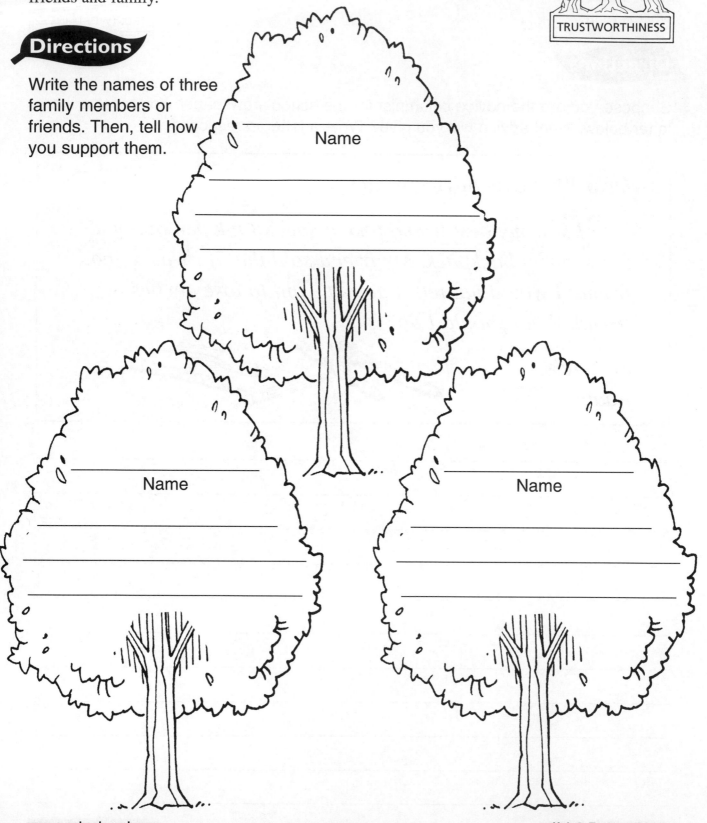

Name

Name

Name

Responsibility

Responsibility is the characteristic that is based on obligation. In a world full of choices, responsibility prompts individuals to be accountable for who they are and what they do. They have a moral duty to follow through and complete a task. It may mean that a person must impose self-restraint to succeed or to persevere if problems arise. Moreover, a responsible person is accountable for decisions—good or bad.

The basic qualities of responsibility include:
- Know what you are to do and do it.
- Think before you act.
- Do your best.
- Keep on trying.
- Be positive.
- Accept the consequences of your choices.

About the Symbol

For students, responsibility often means an obligation to complete a task, such as feeding the dog or picking up toys. At this age, they also need to think about consequences and perseverance. The symbols of the rake and leaves are clearly representative of the work and perseverance aspect, but it should be pointed out to students that without raking, there are consequences of an unsightly lawn and potential problems for harming the spring grass.

About the Story (pages 28–30)

Jordan Waiting by Margaret Countryman
Phoebe wants to go play with her friends instead of taking care of her little brother, who suffered brain damage as a child. But her mother needs Phoebe's help. On the way to the park, Jordan gets lost. He manages to stay calm until Phoebe finds him.

About the Activities

Activity 1: Working at Responsibility (page 31)
Review with students the qualities of responsibility. Help them understand that the word *job* means more than just a task or an assignment. Then, ask students to brainstorm how these qualities relate to the symbol of the leaves and rake. Throughout the course of the unit, remind students to recognize responsible classmates by writing about the actions on the leaves. You may wish to provide a special prize for students whose names appear on the leaves.

Activity 2: Responsibility at Home (page 32)
Explain to students that consequences are the actions that happen after a choice has been made. For example, if a student watches television instead of doing homework, the consequence is that the child gets a poor grade. Then, invite students to tell about jobs they have at home.

Activity 3: Responsibili-Try (page 33)
Lead students in a discussion of attitude and how it affects not only an individual but others as well. Then, brainstorm examples where doing a job is as important as the completed job. (For example, making a cake for a parent. Most parents would be thrilled with the thought, not how it looks!)

Group Project

Invite students to make a Student Responsibility Handbook. Have them pretend that a visitor from another planet has arrived. They need to explain to the visitor the rules of how a responsible student should act. Make a list of students' suggestions. Let each student choose one to illustrate. Bind the pages to make a book.

At-home

Ask students to list on a calendar all their weekly chores and responsibilities. Encourage them to complete each one without being reminded of the task.

Related Reading

...and now Miguel by Joseph Krumgold
Anne of Green Gables by L. M. Montgomery
Call It Courage by Armstrong Sperry

Jordan Waiting
by Margaret Countryman

RESPONSIBILITY

"It's just not fair!" Phoebe Harris wailed. "None of my friends have to watch a babyish little brother."

"I have about an hour of work that must be finished this afternoon," said Phoebe's mother. "End of discussion. I will take care of Jordan tonight. Then you can be with your friends."

"Sometimes being a big sister is just too hard." Phoebe walked out of the room. Then she relented and called to her brother, "Come on, Jordan. Let's go!" It was no use arguing any more. Phoebe knew that she had to take care of Jordan. Her mother depended on her.

"Jordan, you must stay with your sister at the park," said Mrs. Harris. "Use your head. Be smart," she added.

When Jordan was a baby, he was very sick. His lungs had become infected. He had a high fever for eight days. During part of this time, he was in a coma. As a result, he had some permanent brain damage. His mother felt lucky that Jordan survived at all. She remembered her fear of losing him every time Jordan became ill with a fever and had hallucinations.

"Hurry up, Jordan," Phoebe yelled over her shoulder to her brother. Phoebe marched along a path leading to a large wooded park near their home. Jordan trailed well behind. Sparkles of sunlight reached down through the tree branches. A gentle breeze played in the leaves. Green, yellow, and brown, dark and light, shifted all around Jordan. The movement of the light and colors drew Jordan's attention. He slipped into his own inner world full of color and light.

When Jordan came back to the world of the park, he didn't know where he was. He searched for familiar landmarks, something to help him remember. As seconds became minutes, Jordan grew afraid. He stumbled over to a big rock near a pond. He dropped to the ground next to the rock and cried. Phoebe would be very angry with him.

The sun-warmed rock soothed Jordan. After a time, he stopped crying. Two chipmunks playing around a rotting log froze in their tracks when they spotted the boy. After deciding that he would not harm them, they continued their chase. Jordan thought of his mother. She had often warned him about wandering off. What was it she told him to do if he ever got lost?

"I will wait here for my s-sister to find me," Jordan blurted aloud. This sudden noise caused the chipmunks to seek cover.

A nearby woodpecker, looking for food, caught Jordan's attention. He remembered the bird's tap-tapping from walks with his mother. She often played listening games with him. He came to know the buzz of the "summer bug" and the spring song of the sparrow. He also knew the call of the cardinal and many other sounds. His mother said that the earth sings to us in the voices of her creatures. Jordan listened and waited for Phoebe.

Phoebe was frantic with worry. She had retraced her steps twice, with no sign of Jordan. She decided to go for help. Then she caught sight of a yellow shirt through the trees. With tears streaming down her face, Phoebe raced down the hill. She ran around the pond toward her brother.

Jordan looked up. Phoebe knelt to hug him. Jordan smiled as he announced, "I waited for you."

Think and Talk

What is responsibility? What responsibilities did Phoebe have to her mother and brother?

Story Response

RESPONSIBILITY

Directions

Answer the questions.

1. When Phoebe took Jordan with her to the park, was she being responsible? Explain.

_____

_____

_____

2. Name two consequences that Phoebe faced because she did not watch Jordan.

_____

_____

3. What are two reasons some people will not admit they have done something wrong?

_____

_____

4. Why is it important to think before acting?

_____

_____

_____

5. What are some responsibilities you have at school?

_____

_____

_____

_____

Name _____ Date _____

Working at Responsibility

RESPONSIBILITY

Responsible people know what jobs they are to do, and they do their best to complete them. If responsible people face problems while working, they keep trying until the job is done.

Directions

Look for ways your classmates show responsibility. Write the name of a person on a leaf and tell how the person shows responsibility. Then, hang the leaf on the tree.

Name

Name

Name

Name _____   Date _____

Responsibility at Home

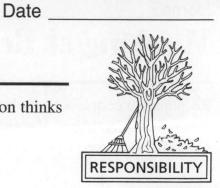

What would happen if a job was not done? A responsible person thinks about how his or her choices affect other people and things.

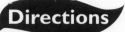 **Directions**

What are three jobs that you have at home? What are the consequences if you don't take care of these responsibilities?

1. Job: _____

_____

_____

_____

2. Job: _____

_____

_____

_____

3. Job: _____

_____

_____

_____

Name _____   Date _____

Responsibili-Try

RESPONSIBILITY

Responsibility is more than just doing a job. It involves the attitude and the process of how the job is done. Sometimes, these two factors are more important than the task being completed.

Directions

Complete each sentence.

1. Think before you act because _____

_____

_____.

2. Do your best because _____

_____

_____.

3. Keep on trying because _____

_____

_____.

4. Be positive because _____

_____

_____.

Directions

Choose one sentence from above. Design a poster featuring your sentence.

Respect

The way to show respect can vary from culture to culture, but this characteristic centers on treating each other and ourselves with consideration and dignity. The primary thought is to treat others as you want to be treated—the Golden Rule. This involves using good manners, practicing nonviolence, taking care of others' property, and respecting those who are different.

The basic qualities of respect include:
- Accept differences in others.
- Follow the Golden Rule.
- Respond to anger and insults peacefully.
- Use good manners.
- Be polite.

About the Symbol

Most students know of the Golden Rule— "Do unto others as you would have them do unto you." But at this age, students are beginning to form social groups based on interests and other identity factors. It is the ideal time for them to learn about and practice tolerance for those who are different. The different trees symbolize that there are many different trees in a forest, but their uniqueness is what makes the forest interesting and fun to visit.

About the Story (pages 35–38)

Challenge and Change by Mari Burton
Saleem's grandfather is going to live with the family. Saleem considers giving up his bedroom for his grandfather. This means that Saleem would have to share a room with his six-year-old brother. Saleem's respect for his grandfather helps him make the decision.

About the Activities

Activity 1: The Forest of Respect (page 39)
If possible, display pictures of different trees. Point out that there are many different trees in a forest. Discuss how much fun it is to walk in a forest and look at different trees. Then, invite students to compare a forest to their classroom. Guide them to understand that many different people make up the classroom. Brainstorm with students why it is important to have different kinds of people and to accept their differences.

Activity 2: Respect in Sports (page 40)
Lead students in a discussion of what it means to be a good sport. Brainstorm different sports situations, both positive and negative, and talk about how being polite makes for a better team and game.

Activity 3: Respect the Golden Rule (page 41)
Discuss with students the meaning of the Golden Rule. Brainstorm examples of it.

Group Project

Throughout the unit, invite a variety of speakers to visit the class. You might consider those from different backgrounds and cultures, as well as speakers of varying ages. At the end of the unit, have students make posters emphasizing the importance of tolerance and respecting differences.

At-home

Ask students to find ways that family members show respect to each other.

Related Reading

The Hundred Dresses by Eleanor Estes
Racing the Sun by Paul Pitts

Challenge and Change

by Mari Burton

RESPECT

Our house was quiet when I walked inside. I didn't see Mom or Cory. Gramps has been visiting us here in Phoenix, but last week he got sick. Mom had to take him to the hospital. Maybe that's where she was now.

I shut the door behind me. Then I heard Mom talking on the telephone in the kitchen. "Saleem's room would be best. But he loves having his own room, Otis." I knew Mom must be talking to Uncle Otis, her brother in Chicago.

"The doctor said Dad can't live alone any longer. Saleem's bedroom is the only one on the first floor. He'll have to give it up, that's all. Dad can't climb stairs now." I felt a lump in my throat.

There was a long pause. Then I heard Mom again: "No, Otis, you and Vi can't do that. Your apartment is three stories up. Saleem can move back in with Cory. He's six now, you know. Saleem's eleven. It'll be tough on them both, sharing a room, but Dad's entitled to the best home we can give him."

35

I heard Mom say good-bye and hang up the phone. I didn't want her to know I knew what was happening—not yet. I tiptoed back to the front door. I opened it and banged it shut. Then, I called loudly, "Hi, anybody home?"

After supper, we visited Gramps at the hospital. He tried to smile when he saw us, but I could tell he didn't feel like talking. Mom kissed him and tried to bolster his spirits. "We love you, Dad. Remember, the doctor says you'll be fine. We're all here for you."

Our drive home was quiet. Finally, Mom broke the silence. "Gramps can't live alone in New York any longer. He'll have to stay with us." I still didn't let on what I knew. Mom said, "I guess he'll get used to a landscape of sand and cactus. Maybe he'll learn to love it as much as we do!"

Later, in my room, I switched on the small TV Gramps gave me when we got him a bigger set. But I wasn't watching or listening. I was thinking.

Gramps is the greatest, I thought. Until now, he's been active and able-bodied. He loves fishing and other sports. He loves music, too. He sings in the church choir. Mom says he's the best baritone she ever heard.

I thought about having Gramps come to live with us. Most of my thoughts were good. But what about my room? I love having my own place. I have walls for my pennants and posters and a place to be by myself. I especially like not sharing space with my younger brother.

But having Gramps here would be great, too. Gramps has a good sense of humor. We'd get to see him every day, not just on holidays. He won't complain about having to move. I can hear him now: "Challenge and change! That's what life's all about, my boy." He says that a lot. I sat at my desk and wrote down my thoughts. I made two lists. Then I went outdoors to find Mom.

She was in the backyard. "Mom," I said. "I heard what you told Uncle Otis. About my room, I mean." Mom looked worried.

"Well, what do you think? Will you give up your room for Gramps?" she asked.

"I've weighed the pros and cons. That's what Dad always says to do," I told her. Then I smiled. "Looks like the pros won."

Think and Talk

What is respect? How does Saleem show respect in the story?

Name _____   Date _____

Story Response

RESPECT

Directions

Answer the questions.

1. What does Saleem's grandfather mean by the phrase "challenge and change"?

_____

_____

2. What do you think Saleem wrote on his list of cons about sharing a room with his little brother?

_____

_____

3. How will respect help Saleem and his brother solve the problems you identified above?

_____

_____

4. Why is it especially important for younger people to show respect to older people?

_____

_____

5. What are some ways that you show respect in school?

_____

_____

_____

_____

The Forest of Respect

RESPECT

One way to show respect is to accept all people, even if they are different.

Directions

Look for ways your classmates show respect. Write the name of a person on a tree and tell how he or she showed respect. Then, tape the tree in the Forest of Respect.

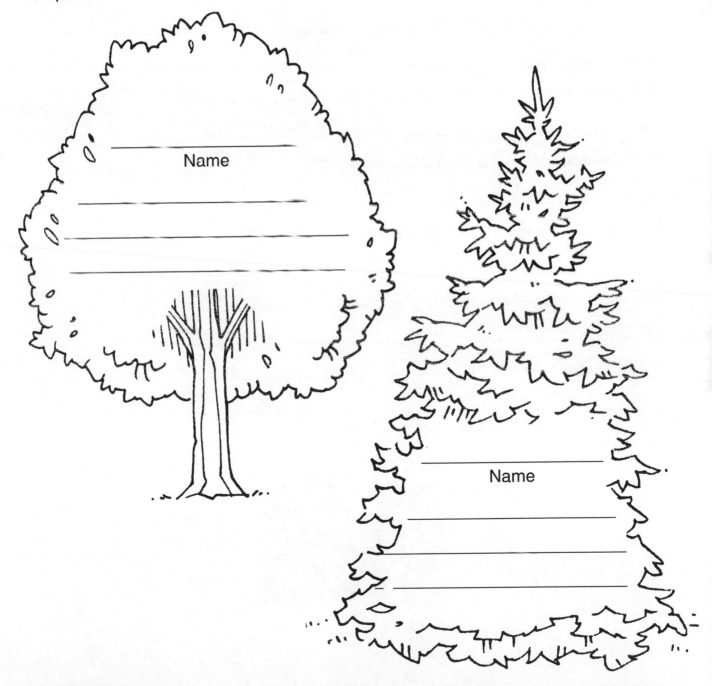

Name

Name

Respect in Sports

RESPECT

People who show respect are polite and use good manners. They say and do nice things wherever they are. Even when playing games, respectful people use their manners. They are good sports!

Directions

Read each situation. Tell what you would say or do to show respect and good manners.

1. A teammate hits a home run. _____

_____

2. A teammate fouls out during her turn at bat. _____

_____

3. A teammate catches the baseball after you call it. _____

_____

4. A player on the other team tags you out as you run to a base. _____

_____

5. A player on the other team calls you a name. _____

_____

6. You score the winning run in a baseball game. _____

_____

Name _____ Date _____

Respect the Golden Rule

RESPECT

One way to show respect is to follow the Golden Rule. The Golden Rule says, *Do unto others as you would have them do unto you.*

Directions

What does the Golden Rule mean? Write it in your own words. Then, draw a picture to go along with it.

_____

_____

_____

_____

Citizenship

We live in a democratic society where freedom and independence are prized and treasured. Citizens have a moral obligation to do their share to honor and improve on these traditions. Citizenship involves making a community better. It can be done by cooperating, obeying rules and laws, voting, and protecting the environment. Moreover, to make wise decisions for these activities, a citizen should learn about the issues.

The basic qualities of citizenship include:
- Work to make the community better.
- Follow laws and rules.
- Be a good neighbor.
- Cooperate.
- Keep the environment safe.
- Learn about activities in the community.
- Vote.

About the Symbol

The community is the focus of citizenship for students at this age. The community includes neighborhoods, businesses, schools, and nature areas. In recent years, society has increased its awareness of the environment, the interdependence between people and the land, and the impact people have on it. The bird is a symbol of nature, and the feeder represents the important role people have in taking care of it.

About the Story (pages 43–46)

The School Mural by Sarah Vázquez
A school is celebrating its fiftieth year, and each class must make a special project. One class paints a huge mural with pictures that represent their school.

About the Activities

Activity 1: Fly High with Citizenship
(page 47)
Lead students in a discussion of citizenship. Ask them how the birds are a symbol of this quality. Lead them to understand that citizenship involves caring for the environment.

You may wish to provide a special treat for students whose names appear on the birds.

Activity 2: News of Citizenship (page 48)
Remind students that a newspaper reporter came to interview the children who painted the mural in *The School Mural*. Brainstorm questions he might have asked. Then, lead students in a discussion of why it is important to learn about the people, activities, and events in a community to make informed decisions. After students complete the activity, you may wish to bind the pages to make a newspaper.

Activity 3: A Citizen's Vote (page 49)
Explain to students that voting is a privilege that people living in a democratic society enjoy. Then, ask students why learning about the candidates is a vital part of the voting process.

Group Project

Discuss with students why it is important to work together to make the community a better place. Then, ask students to think about places around the school campus that need to be improved. Work with school officials to beautify one of those areas.

At-home

Ask students to illustrate at least three rules they follow at home.

Related Reading

Brother Eagle, Sister Sky: A Message from Chief Seattle by Susan Jeffers (illustrator)
The Giver by Lois Lowery
Julie of the Wolves by Jean Craighead George

The School Mural

by Sarah Vázquez

CITIZENSHIP

One morning, Mrs. Sanchez greeted her class. "I have some news. Soon our school will be fifty years old. We're going to have an open house on May twenty-fifth to celebrate this big event."

Mrs. Sanchez said, "Each class will make a big project. It should be about our school and our community."

Paul asked, "What should we do?"

"I'm sure you'll think of some good ideas," said Mrs. Sanchez.

The class went outside for recess. Mei Lee and Paul raced for the swings. They liked to see who could swing the highest.

Mei Lee thought about the big project. She said, "I think we should write a song or put on a play for our class project. What do you think?"

Paul said, "We've done those things. We need a really big project."

While Mei Lee was swinging very high, she looked past the school. She saw the building across the street. It had a big mural painted on the front wall. This gave her a great idea.

Later that day, Mrs. Sanchez asked the class for their ideas. Paul wanted to print a huge banner on the computer. Maria wanted to make bookmarks to give away. Edwina's idea was to make a huge card and have everyone sign it. Mei Lee said, "Let's make a mural."

"What's a mural?" asked Ted.

"It's a big picture painted on the wall of a building," said Mei Lee. "Look at this one at the pet shop." She pointed out the window.

Mrs. Sanchez listed the children's ideas on the board. "These are all good ideas," Mrs. Sanchez said. "Let's pick one that everyone can have a part in. Look over the list again. Then, we'll vote on our project."

Mrs. Sanchez pointed to each idea as they voted. At first, not many children voted. Then, she pointed to the mural idea. Sixteen children raised their hands!

"I think you picked a fine project that everyone can work on," said Mrs. Sanchez.

"Murals are huge! We'll need to think of lots of things to show," said Maria.

Mrs. Sanchez said, "Murals tell about people and their community. Think of some things to tell about our school."

"Let's tell people about our school band," said Beto.

"We'll need a really big wall for our mural," said Maria.

"What about the outside wall we see when we swing on the playground?" asked Paul. "All the classes see it every day!"

Mrs. Sanchez said, "I'll ask our principal, Mr. Ford, if it's OK. Mei Lee, since the mural was your idea, please go with me to see him."

Later, Mrs. Sanchez said, "The principal likes the idea of painting a mural on the wall. He said he will ask if the local newspaper will take a picture of the mural. That would show how our community works together."

Beto asked, "Where will we get the paint? We'll need lots of brushes, too."

Paul said, "Let's ask the art teacher for help. Maybe we could ask our families to help us, too. My mom loves to paint."

"Good idea. Please tell your families about our project, and then I'll call them," said Mrs. Sanchez.

For the next three weeks, the class worked on the mural. First, they planned the scenes to draw. Next, the art teacher helped the children draw sketches of the different scenes on the wall.

Then they started painting the mural. Twenty children couldn't all paint at once, so they took turns. First the band group painted. Then the next

group painted. Some parents helped paint the high parts of the wall near the roof. It was hard work, but everyone had fun.

Some funny things happened. One day, Paul bumped the paint tray and got paint all over himself. Then he slipped and put his hands on the wall. He left his handprints on the mural! Everyone decided it looked good, so they added their handprints, too.

Another time, Anjelina was painting high up on a ladder. She dipped the brush into the bucket and splattered lots of paint onto the wall. But down below her was Beto, so she splattered him, too! He had green hair that day.

When the mural was finished, Mr. Ford called the newspaper. A reporter came to write a story. He asked the class many questions about how they made the mural. He got everyone's name. He took photos of the mural. He told the children to watch for the article soon.

The children could hardly wait to see the article in the newspaper. After about a week, the article appeared with a big photo of the mural. The headline said, "Children Show School Pride."

On the day of the open house, Mr. Ford spoke to all the children, parents, and visitors. He told everyone what project each class had done. Then he invited the visitors to walk around and see all the projects. The children were very proud and excited.

When Mr. Ford told about the mural, the crowd cheered. One neighbor stood up and thanked the students for making such a beautiful painting. He said people would enjoy it for many years.

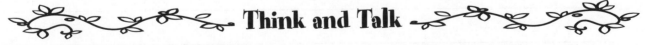

Think and Talk

What is citizenship? What are some examples of citizenship in the story?

Story Response

CITIZENSHIP

Directions

Answer the questions.

1. How did the mural make the community a better place?

   _____

   _____

2. What is cooperation? Name three ways the people in the story cooperated.

   _____

   _____

3. How do people find out about activities and events in your community?

   _____

   _____

   _____

   _____

4. Why is it important for everyone to follow laws and rules?

   _____

   _____

   _____

   _____

5. What kinds of pictures would you paint on a mural to represent your school?

   _____

   _____

   _____

Name _____   Date _____

Fly High with Citizenship

Good citizens cooperate to get a job done. They work together as a team.

 **Directions**

Look for ways your classmates cooperate. Write the name of a person on a bird and tell how he or she cooperated. Then, put the bird on the tree.

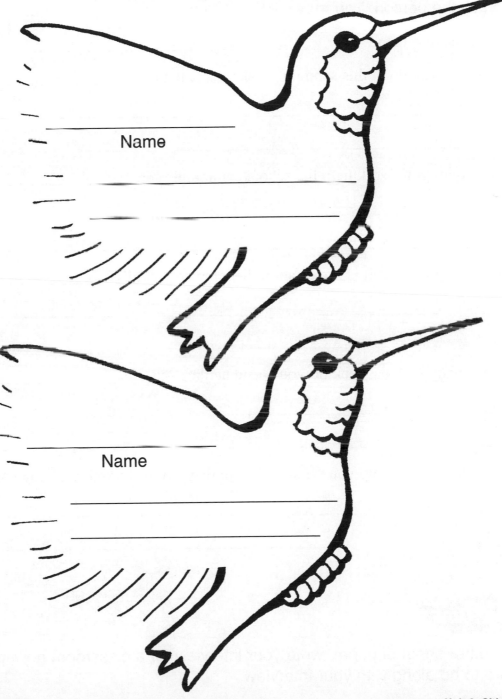

Name

Name

Name _____   Date _____

News of Citizenship

Responsible citizens learn about people, activities, and events in the community. Being informed helps citizens make thoughtful decisions about their community and themselves

CITIZENSHIP

Directions

Imagine that you are a school newspaper reporter. Think of a student, teacher, or volunteer who makes your school a better place. Use the questions below to interview the person. You may wish to add questions of your own.

1. What is your name? _____

2. What do you do in this school to make it a better place? _____

_____

_____

3. How does your work help the school community? _____

_____

_____

4. Why do you think it is important to help the community? _____

_____

_____

5. How many hours a week do you spend helping others? _____

_____

_____

6. Do other people help you? If so, who are they? How do you work together? _____

_____

_____

Directions

On another sheet of paper, write your interview for a classroom newspaper. Draw a picture to go along with your interview.

Name _____   Date _____

A Citizen's Vote

CITIZENSHIP

People vote to choose who will make the rules in a community. It is important for citizens to learn about who those people are and what ideas they have to improve the community.

Directions

Two students are running for president of the Student Council. Read about each candidate.

Ben gets to school early every day. He helps the librarian by shelving books and finding special books for teachers. He even helps students do research on the computer. Once a week, he reads books to a first-grade class. Ben wants to raise money to buy more books for the library.

Jan likes to play basketball. During outside free time, she forms teams to play a basketball game. She makes sure everyone gets to play. If students get angry during the game, Jan helps them solve the problem. She wants to find a way for students to stay after school to play if they want to.

Directions

Which candidate would you vote for? Explain.

_____

_____

_____

_____

_____

_____

_____

Wrapping Up

Some of the character traits, like caring, are easy for students to understand, identify, and practice. Some of the character traits, such as trustworthiness, are more intrinsic, and therefore, harder for students to conceptualize. Learning about each individual character trait is important. But in reality, many of the character traits overlap. When there is caring, there is usually respect. When there is responsibility, there is often trustworthiness. The final unit develops the concept that many of the character traits intertwine and are important to live a healthy, moral life.

About the Story (pages 51–54)

The Crane Wife retold by Ena Keo

In this Japanese tale, a poor man wishes for a wife. On the way home, he finds a hurt crane and nurses it back to health. A wife appears at his door shortly afterward. She weaves beautiful silk cloth to help him earn money. The man's greed for the beautiful cloth and the money it brings him causes his downfall.

About the Activities

Activity 1: Stories That Show Good Character (page 55)

Review all six character traits and the qualities associated with each. Encourage students to share examples of each. Then, brainstorm movies, books, and television shows in which characters exemplify the traits.

Activity 2: Puzzled About Character (page 56)

Review the character traits and the qualities associated with each.

Activity 3: Good Character Autobiography (page 57)

Remind students that a biography is a story written about the life of a real person. An autobiography is a story that someone writes about his or her own life. Then discuss the elements of a persuasive letter.

Activity 4: Questions About Character (page 58)

Now that students have completed all the units, have them choose two of the targeted character traits and then interview a person who exemplifies these traits.

Activity 5: Showing Good Character (page 59)

Students should have completed several of these forms throughout the course of the character education program. Have students select examples of their best work and collect them in a decorated folder. The cover of the folder may be decorated with drawings or magazine pictures that show people demonstrating respect, citizenship, caring, or other positive character traits.

Activity 6: Character Calendar (page 60)

You may wish to plan a final group project in which the whole class selects a character trait to work on each day. The students then use the character calendar to record the trait chosen and how they exhibited the trait throughout the day.

Group Project

Help students plan a celebration of good character. Have them display their group projects from the previous units. For those projects completed outside the classroom, ask volunteers to draw pictures or write about the activities.

At-home

Have students make an invitation to the class celebration to take home to family members.

Related Reading

Shiloh by Phyllis Reynolds Naylor
Sing Down the Moon by Scott O'Dell

The Crane Wife

retold by Ena Keo

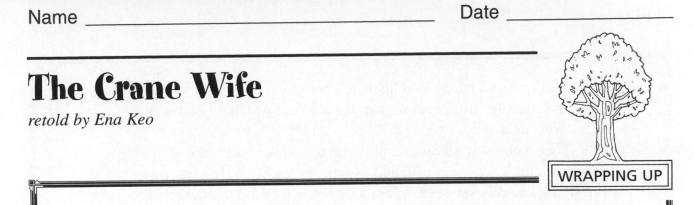

As Sachi was walking home one night, a strong wind was blowing. Snow was coming down hard. He hurried to get home where it was warm. But there was not a wife waiting there for him.

Sachi felt so lonely. He made a wish for a wife. Suddenly, he heard a soft cry in the dark. He walked toward the sound. He found a beautiful white crane that had been hurt. "Don't be afraid. I'll help you," said Sachi.

Sachi carefully picked up the crane and carried it home. He gently cared for its broken wing. He kept it safe and warm until it grew strong and was able to fly again. Then one day, the beautiful white crane flew away.

Later, there was a knock at Sachi's door. He opened it to see a beautiful woman standing there. She bowed and smiled as if she knew Sachi. Then she asked him if she could be his wife. Sachi's wish for a wife had been granted.

Sachi was very thankful that the woman had come to him. He had waited a long time for a wife. Yukiko was her name. She was gentle and graceful. She was also very kind to Sachi.

After many months, Sachi could not find any work. He had no money. Sachi did not know what to do. Yukiko said she could help. She told him she could weave beautiful silk to sell.

Sachi was so happy that his wife could help. Yukiko said, "I will begin to weave the silk. But promise that you will not watch when I weave."

"Yes, dear wife, I promise," Sachi said.

Then Yukiko went away and began to weave. Later, she showed her silk to Sachi. It was beautiful and as light as feathers. He said it was the finest silk he had ever seen. Sachi took the silk to the market to sell.

The silk sold for a very high price. "I'm lucky to have such a clever wife," said Sachi.

He used the money to buy fine paintings and fancy new clothes. Sachi felt important in his new silk kimono. He liked having money. He asked Yukiko to weave more silk for him.

Yukiko wove more silk for Sachi. He kept his promise and did not watch her weave. Each time Yukiko wove silk, it was even more beautiful than the time before.

Sachi's silk was different from the rest. Everyone at the market wanted to buy it.

Sachi asked Yukiko to weave more and more silk. Sachi grew rich. But Yukiko grew very pale and tired.

Before long, Sachi had spent all of his money. He went to Yukiko and asked her to weave silk again. Sachi said, "I promise, this is the last time I will ask. I will save this money."

Yukiko asked Sachi to repeat his promise to save the money. She also reminded him of his promise not to watch her weaving. Then Yukiko set to work. Click, clack, click, clack went the loom all night long.

Sachi grew tired of waiting for Yukiko to finish weaving. He waited as long as he could. Finally, Sachi could not wait any longer. He had to see how his wife was weaving the beautiful silk. He opened the doors to Yukiko's room. He saw a beautiful white crane weaving silk on a loom!

Sachi couldn't believe his eyes. Yukiko was really the crane he had saved! The crane cried out, "You said that you would not watch me weave. Why did you break your promise?"

The crane sighed, "Now I must leave you." She lifted her wings and flew out the door. Sachi knew it was too late. He had driven her away.

Many lonely weeks passed for Sachi. It would soon be spring in the village. The cherry blossoms were in bloom. Everyone was happy except for poor, lonely Sachi. Every day, he searched the sky for the beautiful white crane. He never did find her.

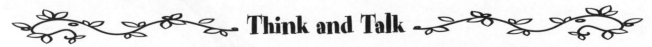

Think and Talk

What are some ways Sachi and Yukiko show good character? Do they always act as they should?

Story Response

Directions

Answer the questions.

1. How does Sachi show citizenship?

_____

_____

2. Is Sachi fair to Yukiko? Explain.

_____

_____

3. How does Sachi break Yukiko's trust?

_____

_____

4. What are the consequences of Sachi's actions?

_____

_____

5. What is greed? How does it change people?

_____

_____

_____

_____

Name _____ Date _____

Stories That Show Good Character

Directions

Name the character trait shown by the symbol. Then, name a character from a book, movie, or television program who shows that trait.

1. _____

_____

_____

_____

2. _____

_____

_____

_____

3. _____

_____

_____

_____

4. _____

_____

_____

_____

5. _____

_____

_____

_____

6. _____

_____

_____

_____

Puzzled About Character

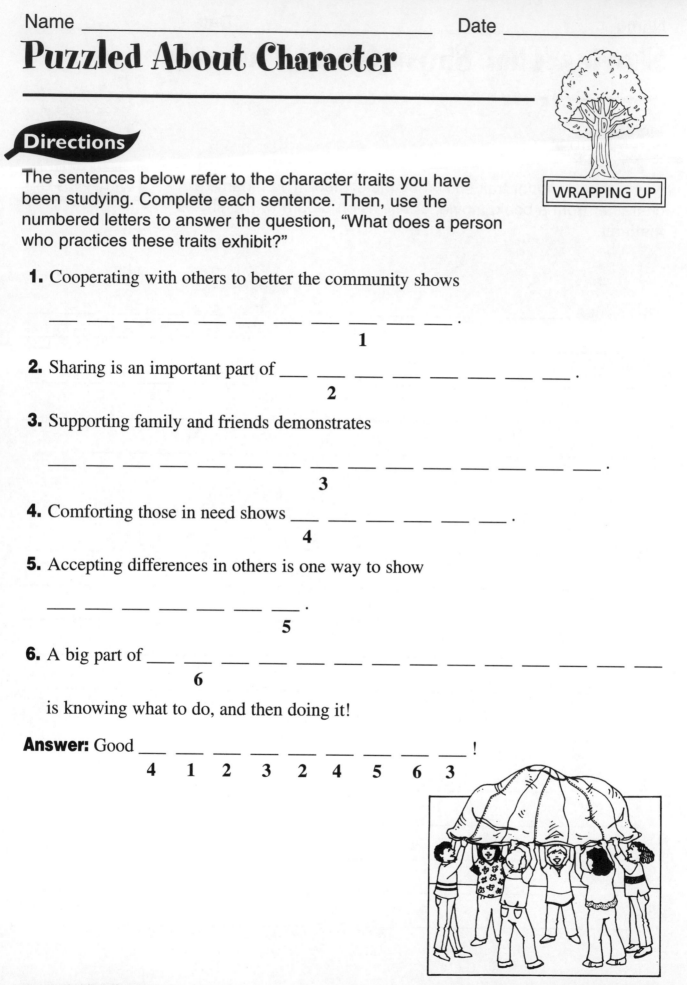

WRAPPING UP

Directions

The sentences below refer to the character traits you have been studying. Complete each sentence. Then, use the numbered letters to answer the question, "What does a person who practices these traits exhibit?"

1. Cooperating with others to better the community shows

___ ___ ___ ___ ___ ___ ___ ___ ___ ___ ___ ___ .
　　　　　　　　　　　　1

2. Sharing is an important part of ___ ___ ___ ___ ___ ___ ___ ___ .
　　　　　　　　　　　　　　　　　　2

3. Supporting family and friends demonstrates

___ ___ ___ ___ ___ ___ ___ ___ ___ ___ ___ ___ ___ .
　　　　　　　　　3

4. Comforting those in need shows ___ ___ ___ ___ ___ ___ .
　　　　　　　　　　　　　　　　　　4

5. Accepting differences in others is one way to show

___ ___ ___ ___ ___ ___ ___ .
　　　　　　5

6. A big part of ___ ___ ___ ___ ___ ___ ___ ___ ___ ___ ___
　　　　　　　　6

is knowing what to do, and then doing it!

Answer: Good ___ ___ ___ ___ ___ ___ ___ ___ ___ !
　　　　　　　 4　1　2　3　2　4　5　6　3

Good Character Autobiography

WRAPPING UP

Directions

Think about a time that you showed each character trait. Write a brief description about the event or activity.

Caring: _____

_____

Fairness: _____

_____

Trustworthiness: _____

_____

Responsibility: _____

_____

Respect: _____

_____

Citizenship: _____

_____

Directions

Suppose the community was giving out an award to students who had shown good character. On your own paper, write a letter to the committee telling why you should get the award. Use the information above to write your letter.

Name _____ Date _____

Questions About Character

Think of someone you admire. Ask that person the questions below to find out how he or she shows the character trait your teacher names.

Character Trait: _____

1. What does this character trait mean to you?

_____

_____

_____

2. How have you shown this character trait to others?

_____

_____

_____

_____

3. When has someone shown this character trait to you?

_____

_____

_____

_____

Showing Good Character

Directions

Complete the paragraphs to tell how you showed good character.

On _____ , I showed the character trait of

_____ .

Here is what I did:

_____

_____

_____ .

It made me feel _____

because _____

_____

_____ .

Next time I would _____

_____

_____

_____

_____

_____

_____

_____ .

Name _____ Date _____

Character Calendar

Month: _____ Dates: _____

Monday
_____
_____
_____

Tuesday
_____
_____
_____

Wednesday
_____
_____
_____

Thursday
_____
_____
_____

Friday
_____
_____
_____

CARING AWARD

Congratulations,

You showed the character trait of

C A R I N G

when you

Sincerely,

FAIRNESS AWARD

Congratulations,

You showed the character trait of

F A I R N E S S

when you

Sincerely,

TRUSTWORTHINESS

AWARD

Congratulations, _____!

You showed the character trait of
T R U S T W O R T H I N E S S
when you _____

_____

Sincerely,

_____

RESPONSIBILITY

AWARD

Congratulations, _____!

You showed the character trait of
R E S P O N S I B I L I T Y
when you _____

_____

Sincerely,

_____

RESPECT

AWARD

Congratulations,

_____!

You showed the character trait of
R E S P E C T
when you

_____

_____

Sincerely,

_____

CITIZENSHIP

AWARD

Congratulations,

_____!

You showed the character trait of
C I T I Z E N S H I P
when you

_____

_____

Sincerely,

_____

Character Education Grades 5–6

Answer Key

p. 8

1. Considerate means thinking about the rights and feelings of others. Quan was careful not to embarrass Travis about not having money or time to play baseball. He found a way to help Travis join the team and keep his pride.
2. Charity is given without expecting anything in return. The team helps Travis so he can earn money for a uniform on his own as well as have time to do something he enjoys.
3. Possible responses: taking food to a sick person; telling someone thank you; listening to a friend's problems
4. Possible response: We all depend on one another, and everyone should help others when they are able to.
5. Answers will vary.

p. 11

Answers may vary slightly. There are three inconsiderate acts:

1. Two girls are talking about another girl who may not be as well off financially.; The two girls should accept the girl as she is and try to get to know her.
2. Two boys run into each other, causing one to spill a tray of food.; The boys can apologize and work together to clean up the mess.
3. One boy is cutting in line.; He should apologize and go to the end of the line or ask permission to cut.

p. 15

1. The African-American children had inferior schools, books, and materials.
2. Thurgood Marshall was the first African American to sit on the court.
3. Prejudice is an opinion formed ahead of time or before all facts are known.; A prejudiced person does not think about new ideas and will not give others a fair chance.
4. Possible response: If someone receives an equal opportunity, then that person has a fair chance of achieving his or her goals.
5. Answers will vary.

p. 17

1. Do not take advantage of people.
2. Be open-minded and listen.
3. Do not blame people carelessly.
4. Take turns and share.
5. Treat people equally.

p. 23

1. Tell the truth.; Do what is right, even if it is hard to do.
2. No, because this was a secret that harmed other people. Also, she wanted money to keep the secret.
3. Secrets that are about surprises or confidences that do not harm others should be kept. Some examples are: presents, special events or parties, or personal information a friend or family member shares.
4. Secrets that affect other people in a bad way should be shared with parents, teachers, or police officers.
5. Answers will vary.

p. 30

1. No, because she did not have a positive attitude nor did she do her best.
2. Possible responses: She loses Jordan, and she has to go look for him.
3. Possible responses: The person does not want to get in trouble or is embarrassed.
4. Possible response: You can imagine a variety of outcomes and choose the best possible action.
5. Answers will vary.

p. 38

1. New and different situations present challenges that people must deal with, often resulting in a change in the person.
2. Possible responses: no privacy; different bedtimes; have to take down pennants and posters
3. They will be more patient and understanding of each other.
4. Answers will vary but should show the students recognize the value of what older people can teach them.
5. Answers will vary.

p. 40

1–6. Answers will vary. Accept reasonable answers that show support or ignore poor sportsmanship.

p. 46

1. Possible responses: It was much more interesting to look at than a plain wall.; People worked together to make something beautiful.
2. Possible responses: Cooperation is when a group of people work together to accomplish a task.; Parents helped paint. The children took turns painting.; The art teacher helped draw the pictures.
3. Possible responses: newspaper, television, radio, fliers, billboards, word-of-mouth
4. Possible response: If people did not follow rules, they could do whatever they wanted to do. It might hurt people in the community.
5. Answers will vary.

p. 54

1. He cares for the crane when it is hurt.
2. No, because he keeps taking advantage of her by asking her to weave more silk.
3. He watches her weave after he has promised not to.
4. The crane must leave, so he loses his beautiful wife.
5. Greed is a selfish desire to have more than what is needed. Greed causes people to forget what is really important.

p. 56

1. citizenship
2. fairness
3. trustworthiness
4. caring
5. respect
6. responsibility
Answer: Good character!

CARING

CARING

- Help and comfort those in need.
- Be kind and considerate to all.
- Thank those who do a kindness.
- Forgive those who are mean or thoughtless.
- Give to others in time and money—charity—to make their life better.

FAIRNESS

FAIRNESS

- Take turns and share.
- Treat people equally.
- Be open-minded and listen.
- Do not blame people carelessly.
- Do not take advantage of people.
- Let consequences fit the wrongful act.

TRUSTWORTHINESS

TRUSTWORTHINESS

- Support your family and friends.
- Tell the truth.
- Do what you say you will do.
- Be on time.
- Keep secrets that do not harm others.
- Do what is right, even if it is hard to do.

RESPONSIBILITY

RESPONSIBILITY

- Know what you are to do and do it.
- Think before you act.
- Do your best.
- Keep on trying.
- Be positive.
- Accept the consequences of your choices.

RESPECT

RESPECT

- Accept differences in others.
- Follow the Golden Rule.
- Respond to anger and insults peacefully.
- Use good manners.
- Be polite.

CITIZENSHIP

CITIZENSHIP

- Work to make the community better.
- Follow laws and rules.
- Be a good neighbor.
- Cooperate.
- Keep the environment safe.
- Learn about activities in the community.
- Vote.

DOMINOES

CITIZENSHIP		CITIZENSHIP		CITIZENSHIP	
RESPECT		RESPECT		RESPECT	
RESPONSIBILITY		RESPONSIBILITY		RESPONSIBILITY	
TRUSTWORTHINESS		TRUSTWORTHINESS		TRUSTWORTHINESS	
FAIRNESS		FAIRNESS		FAIRNESS	
CARING		CARING		CARING	

DOMINOES

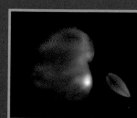 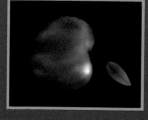 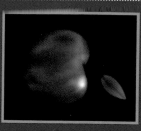

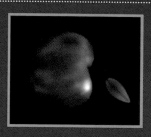 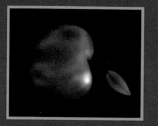 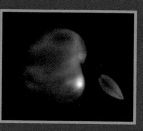

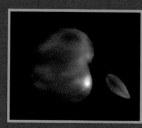 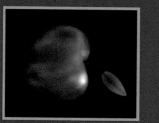 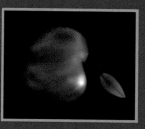

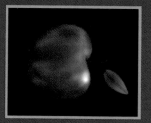 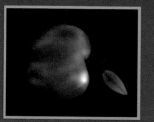 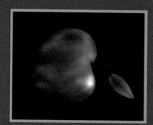

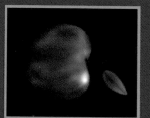 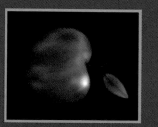 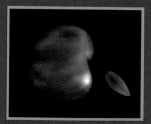

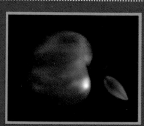 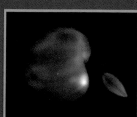 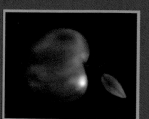

DOMINOES

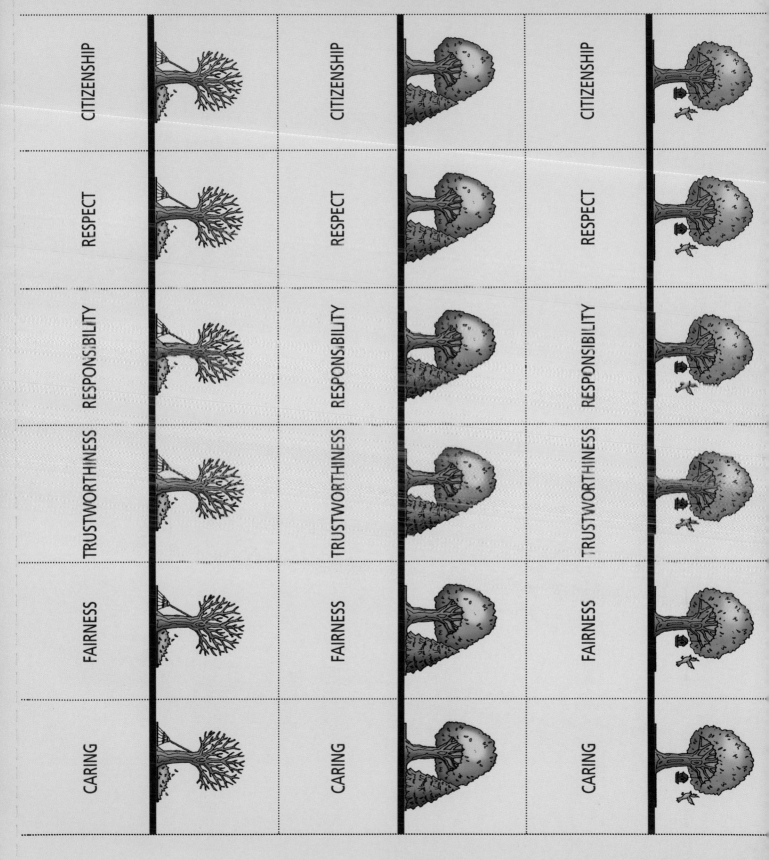

CITIZENSHIP	CITIZENSHIP	CITIZENSHIP
RESPECT	RESPECT	RESPECT
RESPONSIBILITY	RESPONSIBILITY	RESPONSIBILITY
TRUSTWORTHINESS	TRUSTWORTHINESS	TRUSTWORTHINESS
FAIRNESS	FAIRNESS	FAIRNESS
CARING	CARING	CARING

DOMINOES

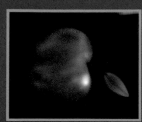
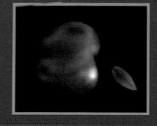
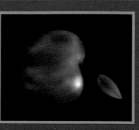
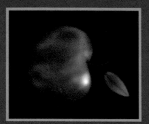
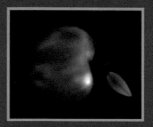
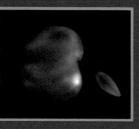
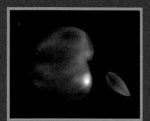
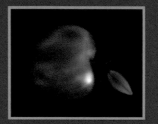
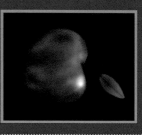
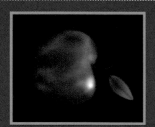
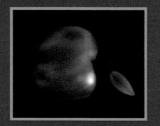
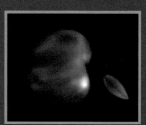
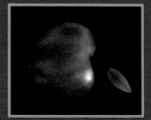
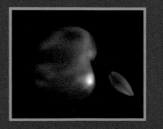
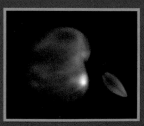
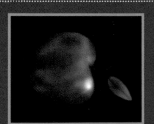
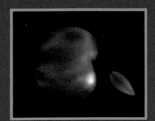
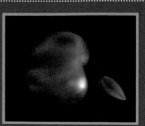